D0865286

Notwithstanding

Poems

Brit Washburn

Wet Cement Press
Berkeley, California

ISBN: 978-1-7324369-5-4

Wet Cement Press
Berkeley, California
www.wetcementpress.com

Cover drawing by Matt Sullivan

Acknowledgments:
Thank you to the editors of the following
publications in which some of these poems
first appeared: *Alexandria Quarterly*, *ArtMag*,
Culture Keeper & *What Matters*.

With gratitude to my beloved parents and
children, and to the poet Nick Bozanic,
whose lives are all part of this work.
Thank you to Holly Wren Spaulding, Lisa
Wells and Barbara Roether for their ongoing
solidarity in the trenches of poetry. Thanks
to Thoreau Lovell & the editors at Wet
Cement Press for their careful attention, and
to Stephen Dunn and the Vermont Studio
Center. Finally, to Matt Sullivan,
thank you in advance.

WCP5-2

Contents

You said, though your own heart condemn you

I do not condemn you.

—Franz Wright

We were not born to survive, only to live.

—W. S. Merwin

Harvest

On the kitchen counter, three ripe tomatoes
a heap of sweet onions, a pile of potatoes

caked with dirt, but sacred for that,
like hands calloused from work, or the skin's

star chart of scars—here, where the nail went in,
here the dog's teeth, here the knife;

here, where the scalding water spilled, here,
where the car door slammed closed; here

where our children grew ripe like fruit,
here, where your mouth named the hurt—

faint now, like the taste of rain in wine,
or the sense of something missing,

or the memory of our bodies
as gardens before the harvest.

Part I: Coupling

Lentamente

The quality of light tells us
it is early still—grayer than gold,
colder than it will be once the sun
rises above the tree line, descends
at a sharper angle
through the window above
the bed where we have slept
the sleep of innocents.

There is time yet
to keep our eyes closed,
feel the air move over
our bodies like the spirit
over the deep, long hours
filled with stillness, and motions
chosen carefully, carelessly
as words, the back of your hand
run along my arm from wrist
to shoulder—slowly, but with
precision like a bow over strings,
or the brush scrape you use
to make a cymbal shiver to life,

a knife slicing through the ripe
flesh of a peach, sweetness
earned by patience, the first kiss
months after meeting and brief,

the next, weeks later, or so it seemed,
as if there were no hurry, as if
we had our entire lives ahead of us,
which we do, though we are all, always,
as young as we'll ever be, and
hungry.

Double Sonnet
on a Singular Soup

Every hour, the broth's body
boldens, from nothing but a bit
of oil in water, to vaguely
aromatic—an infusion of parsley
and peppercorn, underneath onion,
carrot, celery and
a suggestion of thyme.

Not yet soup, not yet
a medium for chick peas and rapini,
whole cloves of garlic sautéed
and stirred in just before serving
with crostini and Sangiovese
and all our hopes and hungers poised
like a spoon before the other's mouth—

Too hot to taste, too fragrant
to resist and so we blow, gently,
our breath rippling the liquid's surface,
and we sip, gingerly, our lips
pursed, our eyes closed as though
to tune all else out, wanting to know
only this moment: so long

in coming, so quick
to pass, so impossible

to reproduce or recollect—
the second our tongues touch
for the first time
that which we had not realized
we'd been craving all along.

Windfall

We can't believe our luck:
to have found this
pair of pears on the ground
in the grass, in the abandoned
orchard late in the year, spared
as if by fate, unmarred and,
we tell ourselves, ours.

Furtively, we seize them,
glancing sidelong like thieves,
rubbing them against our shirts,
our palms, inhaling the faint
perfume of their ripeness before
biting in—like savages, we imagine,
though imagining makes us not,
makes us the self-conscious creatures
we are, knowing full-well
we have done nothing to earn this,
do not deserve it, but that
the pleasure we take makes us
worthy of taking, our happiness
a form of gratitude, refusing grace
a blasphemy more grave than greed.

Left alone, they would go to waste.
Kept for later they would bruise and rot.
Now is the only time for joy. Here

the only place. And you, My Love,
are the only one—so let us eat, and praise,
and walk among these gnarled trees
before we lie beneath them.

Sacred Geometry

for A.

In your absence I picture
your calloused palms—the small,
raw patches of skin
where blisters have torn
open beneath a rake-
handle or stake-driver,
how they feel when I run
my lips along them.

I sweep the hay
that fell from your cuffs
when you took your pants off
in the kitchen and am tempted
to save it, as I have the spider-
wort blossom you brought to me
in a jewelry box—a pale
amethyst bud inside
a dark amethyst sheath, placed
beside a candle on the table.

It is a kind of idolatry, this
worship of relics, of detail,
where the devil is said to be,
but blasphemy, too,
to ignore the sacred

geometry of our bodies
which fit together
like the parts of flowers.

Pythagoras believed
that harmonic ratios—the perfect
fourth, and the perfect fifth—gave music
the power to cure, to harmonize
an out-of-balance mind, as you have
mine, reminding me
of the privilege of work, the honor
of feeding a herd, the daily
redemption of a hot shower
shared, a warm meal
of soup and bread, and a bed
where the rites of love tire us
so thoroughly we sleep as if
delivered from this life
and wake in the morning
as if reborn to it: in awe
of sunlight and fresh fruit
and the sight of one another
naked, perfectly imperfect
as the earth.

Om

for Ess

What if, as the yogis supposed
of heartbeats and breaths,
we each had only
a finite number
of words at our disposal
before the final silence?

                                   What

would I say to you then? What
could not be gestured, conveyed
by kissing your eyelids, bowing
my head and tucking it in
beneath your wing as if we were
one bird, turning in for the night
and safe, so safe

we open to one another
in the light of day, exposed
as only those most certain
of nothing but death
and yet determined to live
can bear to be.

                                  What then

would I utter but this
moan of hopeless devotion,
of supplication and surrender,

which is the sound the body makes
when it comes to life or leaves it—
the first cry, the last poem spoken.

Epiphany

When we finish, I lie still in the candle's glow
and watch you sleep: your face relaxed,
your skin lit up like honey in the sun,
your mouth more beautiful than I can comprehend.

In the evening's perfect silence, your breath
deepens to the low roar they say
kept bears away from caves and somehow
makes me feel safe even now.

I slip away to make our dinner—brown rice
and vegetables sautéed with ginger, sesame,
lemongrass; green tea in a glass pot, mineral water
in mason jars, an amaryllis blooming on the table.

Earlier, we drove to see paintings
in the capitol, jerseys at a dairy in Bowman,
their udders full, their eyes clear
and content in the bleak January twilight.

Poem on the Summer Solstice

The longest day of the year, we're told,
as though time could be measured
in hours of light and did not expand
with suffering, contract with happiness:
interminable minutes in hospitals and factories,
courtrooms and queues, the brevity
of every second I've spent with you—

Never long enough to accommodate
all that we would talk about, all
that we would taste and touch:
the year's first sweet corn cut
from the cob, each kernel a capsule
containing the savor of every summer
that ever was, resurrecting our child-
hoods as though they were not gone
for good, as though we could recover
a sense of wonder, of trust, blind faith
in the endlessness of seasons, of love,
possibilities boundless and abundant
as dandelions and damselflies,
lazy afternoons by a lake we've yet to learn
is deep enough to drown in, but too shallow
for diving off the dock, the bottom rocky
and strewn, too, with small stones
skipped across the surface, then sunk,
each one a wish we came to know

would come to naught, but kept throwing
anyway, little offerings to the water god
whose altar lies beneath these waves
of memory, washing over us as we attempt
to fathom where on earth the time went,
and where it might go next.

Banana Bread

I felt such affection for you lying there in bed,
read the subject line of a message
which itself had no content,
and yet it said enough
to get me up and dressed,
and into the kitchen to bake for you
banana bread—one among the emblems
of affection I offer,
in hopes of making up
in earnestness and perseverance
for the grandeur that my gestures lack.

Love, I would wager, is like that:
an effort to express
except in bits and pieces,
fits and starts, drops of water
in a pail which even still may get
tipped over, knocked down, forcing us
to begin again, more gingerly,
this time, knowing
how precariously balanced it is,
how fragile, how at risk, and these small acts
our only defense.

And so once more
I gather the ingredients,
measure them carefully, and do my best

to turn the bygone fruit
into a thing of comfort—
sweet and warm and filling;
familiar, familial, redolent
of what it is you want,
what you've always wanted,
what was almost lost.

Part II: Parting

Unlikeness

This apple has nothing to do with you
or me or love or loss. Unlike us,
it is perfect, golden and blushing
and exquisitely shaped, miraculous
just sitting there, on the cutting board
beside the forged steel knife;
more beautiful still when I slice it
in half, the skin splitting with a snap,
the flesh bright white and glistening,
the tear-shaped seeds in their
heart-shaped sheathes exposed.

And better yet when I bite into it,
the sweetness like a kiss, the crispness
like fall itself, the tart the counterpart
that gives all lovely things
their resonance, like silence and absence
and darkness and pain—

But we're talking about an apple here,
and if there's nothing more to say of it
(it's finished, after all), then let us turn
our attention to the dripping
faucet: Its arc like the neck of a swan,
the water dropping metronomically
into a bowl of itself, which has long-
since overflowed, though slowly,

like those infinity pools you see
sometimes whose surfaces seem
to meet the ether as the sea and sky
meet at the horizon—seamlessly, easily,
entirely.

Caesura

The conditions could not have been better:
a summer evening, cooler than usual;
a sidewalk cafe, at the end of the day.
Intimations of rain, but nothing threatening;
hard subjects broached, and out of the way.

We sat side by side at the table,
shared a glass of wine, watched the passersby:
women in heels too high for their legs, men
dressed identically in polos and khakis—

Some caroused; others
talked softly or, like us, said nothing,
not knowing what would come next—

We'd decided to part ways but seemed
closer for it, more attached, like those sea-
turtles who've been nursed to health
and taken to the beach for release,
who can't bring themselves to leave.

The heart is fickle and the mind is tricky,
but the body simply needs what it needs:
the open ocean and the shore.

And what's wrong with that, finally? Why not
stay a while in the moonlight, allow desire to flood
the hollows, form pools?

Of Being Dispossessed

There are still enough berries here
for both of us this morning,
though I can also eat them all
myself. They are fewer
than before, but more ripe—
dark and sweet and tender
to the tongue.

Eventually, there will be melon, stone fruit,
apples, pears—one season slipping
into the next, like lovers under water
over years.

I've been through this before: I know
how to eat and swim and sleep alone,
how to savor a sensation without sharing it,
how to carry on.

Time itself won't have it otherwise, careening
headlong as it does,
but death is everywhere in the background—
still and silent in the empty chair; stalking
the garden after dark; lying
on the cool side of the bed.

And the way we spend our days is
the way we spend our lives: together or apart.

I've changed the sheets, aired the room,
slept elsewhere, even, but your pillow
remains here. I wouldn't be rid of it
given the choice, wouldn't trade
this cluttered heart, these laden
boughs, this constant hunger
for the relief of being dispossessed—not yet.

Ghost Love

It's like those ivory-billed woodpeckers
they thought they found in Arkansas,
sixty years extinct: We went searching,
caught sight of something luminous,
and wanted to believe—
                                    And maybe
did believe, dearly, that this could be it—
the broad wingspan, the blue-black plumage,
the white markings and underwings—

But despite *teasing glimpses*
and *tantalizing sounds* no
irrefutable evidence was found,
and what was seen was, most likely,
a common cousin only.
                                    And yet
the male's red crest! the triangular patch
at the small of its back! that distinctive ivory
bill concealing, we could have sworn, a long,
mobile, barbed and hard-tipped tongue; the *kent,
kent* of its drum—
                                    how brutal
to let it go, to concede a close match
is no match at all.

Of Another Season

The first cold morning of fall,
and the house feels emptier for it,
as if someone had slipped away in the night,
left a note on the bedside table—

Let's call her Summer, let's say
she wrote with a graceful slant
that it had been nice while it lasted,
that she appreciated your hospitality,
though you knew she could not stay—

For a while, you served one another—
young lettuces, cucumbers, nasturtiums;
iced tea brewed in the sun—lounged
watching clouds drift and listening to insects
busy themselves in the shrubbery until
your skin was as warm as the honey they made
and you poured yourselves like streams into a lake,
mingling as if to become one body, awhirl
in the deep—

Or so it seemed, though indeed you went
your separate ways, as each of us, even together
in bed, may dream in different directions, and wake
to find we are alone, or in the company of another
season—similar as a sister, but not the same.

After Our Separation

Just over the bridge, to the right
of the road, bales of hay like monoliths,
incongruous, mark your yard: Not yet
a farm, but land with animals who
raise their massive heads and study me,
skeptically, a stranger here.

Their hides are black, their horns curved,
their eyes intelligent, as if, like you, they knew
the work in store, the burdens they will have
to bear to earn their keep, the milk the body
has to weep to pay its debts, collected like rainwater
and turned to drink for other beasts.

We eat our lunch on the back deck—take-out
from a city that feels far away just now.
We pace the property's periphery, lit up
by late-fall sun; you point out deer tracks
in the cornrows, thistles on my boots,
where the neighbors have built blinds.

Midafternoon, the girls lie down and rest
their heaviness against the earth; you
walk me to my car and we come together
as we always have, our mouths and hands
welcoming one another home as though
it were only natural.

And yet, as you've reminded me
time and again, there is nothing natural
about agriculture, even, about domesticating
animals and cultivating crops. Farming,
like love and art, is nature's opposite:
effortful and arduous, if arguably essential.

And everything still goes to seed—weeds
run rampant in fallow fields, surrounded
by pines you vow you'll sell to pay the lease
and clear the view, determined to see the horizon
laid bare before you, unoccluded by useless trees,
the pastoral fallacy; me.

Part III: Tendering

Pure Form

It was summer.
He slept shirtless
between white sheets
and the morning light
through the blinds
made his shape seem
sculptural—
                    like stone,
but warmer, like wood
but so smooth only water
could have wrought the river—
bed of his ribs.

I could not help
but trace each vertebra
with my fingertips, from the nape
of his neck to the downy small
of his back, close my eyes
and feel his breath, rising.

Reconciliation

I wake as if from a bad dream
but have not dreamt, and feel
as if something terrible has happened
though nothing has, yet—

I get up, set the kettle
on the stovetop, slice bread,
lay the table with napkins, plates, jam—

My husband appears,
and one by one our sons;
they climb onto my lap.

I smooth their tangled manes,
kiss their foreheads, push them back—

I cannot bear their chatter,
the complaints and demands—

I give them everything
I can think of, then escape

to the screen porch
where the air is cooler
and our cat, a ginger tabby,
curls up beside me, purring
rhythmically while I sip

my tea and stare out
at the dense, green thicket.

What is wrong with me?
I chose this, and believe in it,
but my heart has forgotten its part—

Look at them:
they are precious. *Teach me,*
my loves, how to love again.

Duplicity

I cannot eat, but I can cook.

I cannot swallow so much
as a mouthful of oats,
but I can simmer them
with cinnamon, honey and milk.

I can slice apples. I can chop nuts.
I can ladle porridge into small cups;
I can wake them up.

I can pack their lunches. I can choose
their clothes. I can send them to school,
I can call them home.

I can make dinner. I can bake bread.
I can bathe them, gently,
and lather their heads.

I can shield their eyes,
I can towel them dry.
I can try.

I can read aloud to them
by lamplight, I can sing them
lullabies. I can even lie down
by their father's side—

But I cannot stop wanting
another life.

Duck Lake at Dawn

In the silence of your soul,
in the bower of your concentration,
the romance with the infinite is endless.
—Paramahansa Yogananda

But first, you must thieve
these moments:

the others asleep, the silence a feast
to devour discreetly, the water's surface

shimmering, glistening, rippling
like a sheet of silk beneath a pair

of Canada geese adrift there; the sky
brightening by degrees

from white to blue to bluer still,
each hue striking a more urgent chord

in the heart's repertoire of desire,
the body's boundless need to drink

it all in: the birch's tattered bark,
the willow's draping limbs,

the memorable geometry of the sedge
whose shape rhymes with its name—

before their breathing deepens,
and they begin shifting in their sleep,

and you are discovered: a flush
in your cheeks, the blood

of solitude coursing—
and there is no denying

the appetite for absence—
voracious, insatiable—

and the incontestable
scarcity of time.

Only an Ungrateful Heart

Only an ungrateful heart despairs
over bickering at the breakfast table
when there is food upon it, a roof above it,
and those around it have their health.

  And yet—who wouldn't rather
clear the dishes and have sex, or walk
out the front door, down the block,
past the strip malls and out of town—
to the streets of Paris, say, or some other
transcendent setting—the dunes
above Lake Michigan, the mountains
around Boulder, Corcovado towering
over Ipanema, the Pali lookout
above Kailua Beach—any place
where you might breathe more deeply,
engage in something—anything—
you wouldn't regret dying during.

  Because it could happen:
This meal could be your last.
So it had better be good—coffee,
fresh berries, a buttery croissant—
and you had better love the object of your
anger— touch his face, trace his lips
while they remain warm with breath,
take him with you when you leave.
For that was the idea: to learn to care
for someone else, without losing yourself,

without *settling for* or *resigning to*
which are sins at least as grim
as ingratitude.
        It is a waste
not to crave beauty, not to feel
the hunger for hunger itself, or even
the knee-buckling sorrow of loss—
privileges all of the living.
        It is spring—
the invisible birds in the marsh
are singing, the azaleas in the front
yard blooming. I've quit my job—
and lost my mind, perhaps.
It's circling now—like the washing machine,
like the earth itself—Thank God.

Cleaving

Is this how the soul feels leaving
the battered, beloved corpse?

Hesitant, eager, guilty—
guilty because it is eager

to go, wishing to blink
and be gone, but forced

to hover

and observe the dying, forcing itself
to bear witness and be sure, look

the body in its glassy eyes,
take its pulse one last time,

kiss the children goodbye
and decide where next and what,

if anything, to take along—
an image or two, a few books,

a sweater and a pair of boots.
This notebook, my favorite cat—

plush, and ashen like the sky,
like the asphalt road

I drove down earlier, music blaring.

Bird Poem

The bird in the road is my heart, it turns out.
It flies up and, in the rear-view mirror, I see it
struck by a truck. Sent hurtling like an apple-
core, it lands on the shoulder, bait
for some hungry scavenger—

I pull over and get out, scan the gravel
and the grass—garbage and squirrel
carcasses, wildflowers and a lost hat.
And then I find it: the small body
still warm—feathers flayed at awkward
angles, beak bloodied, neck snapped limp.

With both bare hands, I scoop it up
and take it back, wrap it
in a muslin rag and place it
on the seat beside me, companion
for the journey. Back

home, the cloth is soaked, and
what's inside has ceased to be
aviary, but has become instead
a lump of clay—damp, malleable,
red—asking to be given

shape again: First wings, and then
a hollow throat through which to sing.

Part IV: Reckoning

As I Lay Waking

Darkness, then
a sliver of light
through the lids
of my eyes, then
darkness again,
thinking better
of opening them.
                Then
a deepening
of breath, a remembering
of limbs, of last
night which ended
only a few
hours ago:
                  Four
in the morning, snow
falling beyond black
windows, beyond
the confines
of a conversation
in a closed room,
the kind that holds
two people captive
to a moment in which,
it seems, they are neither
crazy nor alone
in the suspicion with which
they wake every day:

that all of this is exactly
as it should be, the full
catastrophe—coincidences
and close calls, mistakes
and the mundane which they
must shoulder and suffer
and even praise
for the good fortune
of having been born
to it.

Clarity

And just like that, it's gone
again—the word on the tip
of your tongue, the thought,
the name, the face, the time,
the energy you'd summoned
for a moment, which made everything
make sense—
    The word:
blank, the thought: blank, the name:
blank, the face: blank,
the time, the energy—all
elusive now, as if dreamt,
irretrievable,
    though you go back
to bed, hoping the scent
of the sheets, the tilt
of your head, the darkness
itself might trigger a re-
collection—
    It sounded
like water. It meant
something. You called it
yours. His eyes were
penetrating. The night was
long. You were not
tired.

If the Fog Lifts

after a painting by Megan Aline

In the foreground, a field,
blond and brown but faint
as a bride's long hair
beneath a veil, suggestive,
as is the sky, hovering low
above a small white house
in the middle distance,
awash in mist.

But if the fog were to lift,
the image would resolve:
the edges sharpen, the light distill,
and all would be revealed
for what it is: the field barren,
the house vacant and derelict,
the power lines powerless
to connect anyone with anything.

Yet as it lies, there is a softness—
as if the pastoral still existed, as if,
in the quiet of dusk or dawn,
someone was yawning, cupping
a warm mug in her palms, gazing out
at far-off mountains, humming
Copeland's "Appalachian Spring"
in her head instead of Neil Young's

"Bad Fog of Loneliness;" the children
in bed; the cupboards full, the landscape
virgin, and she herself still in love
with one good man who never left.

God bless fog then: the fog of the Grand
Banks and of Point Reyes, of the Po Valley
and the Swiss Plateau, of London, of course,
and even the fog of war, which is, after all,
nothing more than a phrase to name
the inescapable uncertainty of one's perspective,
no less the case in times of peace: the calm
deceptive, the heather teeming with locusts,
a storm approaching from the East.

The Missing

In the morning, I walk
out in the rain
to look for something
lost, like a woman
out in the rain
looking for something
lost—a key, or
a ring, wondering
how long it takes
for mud to cover
what might have been
apparent in the sun.

But for the rain,
I might not be
so cold, so quick
to give up, to accept
what's gone as gone
and move on—call
a locksmith, grow
accustomed to my own
naked hands.

After all, that's how
they began. And yet
how much easier
to live without
before we've had;

how much more difficult
when something comes
and goes: the stranger
we did not know to miss
turned absence
we can't live with.

Promenade

I wanted to feel stillness
so I went for a walk, watched
the cobblestones pass
beneath my feet, then bricks,
slate, dirt, concrete—

In the square, the grass was burnt
from last week's festival; on the corner,
a man played saxophone
and I wanted to tip him
but had no cash.

It was spring: even the distant
jackhammer seemed harmless
to me in my weariness which returns
like a season itself,
and with it the impulse to flee or retreat,
renounce, stop trying so hard
to keep this life afloat, just let it sink,
soundlessly, to the quiet
bottom of something.

But there were birds, too, if I listened,
and they made me
look up to the soft clouds,
and it is always hard to know
whether they are rolling in

or rolling out; whether the smell
of charred meat in the streets
is gruesome or enticing.

And regardless, you could find,
on the sidewalk, a folded ten-dollar bill,
and feel fortunate, for a moment, as I did,
before wondering how many times I've lost
as much or more, how many times
I will be lost and found again.

April

A couple of weeks of sun and then
it's cold again, a wind in the night
absconding with the infant spring
we thought was ours to keep,
as if seasons or people (our own
minds and bodies, even) were ever
anything but lent to us for foster care,
to love as our own and then release.

For solace: hot tea and Bach—
questions more than answers,
not cold and hard, but liquid
and burning, like what
are we supposed to learn
from nature's fickleness,
and how can we persist
in serving when contingency
renders us skin and bone, no more
transcendent than a stone
worn smooth and mute
by the river's constant coursing.

Watermelon

Every year without fail
bins appear
in the grocery store
and your children beg
for watermelon.

Or someone's selling them
out of the back of a truck on the roadside,
or your childless neighbor,
knowing she won't be able
to go it alone, offers you half,
and brings it over one evening
in June, and you stow it
in the ice box for the night—

And in the morning, you cut
a plateful, and take it
out on the porch with a mug of tea,
and there's a hawk in a tree
across the way, being pestered
by smaller birds, the endless
demands of the world, the minor crises
that must be fielded, but must, also,
be ignored just long enough
to sit down and devour
the sweet, cold pulp of summer
as if for the first time ever,
thinking, *yes, this tastes good,*
if nothing else, this tastes good.

Vagueness

August and overcast—autumnal, almost,
though surely summer isn't finished yet.
Surely we're not yet out of the woods
of heat and steaminess, oppressive
after months the way cold holds siege
in winter.

But then, other seasons are always
greener, meaning *nothing is but thinking
makes it so*. Even variety
affords relief only when it's not
the rule; when it is, we'd give a limb
to be rid of it, to be given instead
a long tall drink of changelessness,
restorative as sleep.

But who hasn't known both
tumult and tedium? And
who could choose between them
any more than between two loves—
if ever such choices were even ours
to make.

Most times, the world comes
prearranged: today the sun
will shine; today, rain; today
something or other will befall us
for good or ill or nothing will,

and we will sit in stillness
and observe the weather
out the window, going nowhere,
slowly, but feeling vaguely aware,
vaguely alive, vaguely alone
and dying, vaguely at home,
vaguely at peace, vaguely restless
and uneasy.

In the Darkness

Again the voice comes that says
*If I must fail, Lord, at least let it be
in private*, quietly, so the defeat won't be
compounded by the witness of it. Another

animal impulse, perhaps, like that
which makes the house cat leave the house
to die, thereby sparing its keepers
the unseemly grasping for breath.

Not to be dramatic. Life goes on and will,
more or less, it's just
so tiresome sometimes, and
as Frost put it, *I'd like to get away*

from Earth awhile. Or at least from people,
with all of their well-meaning hopes for us,
their unspoken expectations, like that we continue
to put one foot in front of the other,

when maybe we'd rather not, maybe
we'd rather step aside, let the others go by,
just close our eyes for a moment
and float in the darkness.

Which reminds me, we never did
make it to that sensory deprivation
chamber you told me about.
It sounded scary, but intriguing, too,

and there's the rub: the one that chafes
the brain on days like this,
existence a coarse robe the mind wears,
and all of us postulants.

But there I go again—
Forgive me. I'll be quiet now.

Even if in Silence

Last night, a dream
of recluse spider bites
along my neck and arms,
beginning to open
and seep like stigmata
and I, methodically
putting my affairs in order
before seeking help,
not wanting to leave
certain things undone:
my children unfed,
letters unanswered,
books unread—

I wake in a sweat,
my skin intact,
my heart pounding
the walls of its cage:
never enough time
to make things right
and already decomposing,
our flesh falling
away from these bones
with more or less gore
and ceremony, but falling
still, even if in silence
and with discretion,

especially if in silence
and with discretion,

like the spiders themselves,
creeping beneath the sheets,
lying in wait, thirsting
for sustenance
like the rest of us.

At Sixty-Three, My Mother

Still equal parts
fire and water,
earth and air, she asks
if we had to choose
between never again sharing
our bed with anyone
or never again sleeping
deeply, deliciously
alone, which would we elect?

Would it be better
never again to hold
and be held, or to be
forever kept too close, touched
too much, as if by beggars
or needy children, their little hands
the pawing claws
of small feral cats,
their mouths the beaks

of ravenous baby birds,
obscenely open, cheeping
incessantly, insistently,
like the voices in our heads
or the very voice of God
we wouldn't be rid of
but nor can we bear

to go on hearing,
moon after moon,

though we can't know,
either, what goes on
after: the chorus
of questions unanswered,
or the deafening
silence, the longing
to be braided with one other
body, or the need to be
let be.

Part V: Cleaving

Missive from a Distance

How can I show you
what I have left you to find?
The way the road winds
across the countryside—slack—
then tangles around cities, then frees
itself again, like line from a fish's lip.

Sometimes it is the hook that gets caught,
rips off, and the fish swims on—

But I have no business writing fish poems
—that is your jurisdiction—even though
you are at home in mine: the kitchen
and the bath; the bedside—tending
our children in those spaces I inhabited
so thoroughly I vanished and was no longer there.

Still, I care. Tell them so, if you can bear to,
tell them their mother remains and will return,
tell them the road doubles back like a river;
ask them to forgive me, as I ask you, as I have
my own mother, finally, after twenty-five years.

For she, too, lost her grip and slipped
the surly bonds of earth to touch the face
of nothing save her own mirror image,
a clock keeping time, lines unreeling
as from a skein of filament—scarcely visible—

but resistant as eight-pound test, the weight
of a newborn babe.

What I wanted to say is that
you'd like it here—the cloud-
shrouded mountains surrounding
the highway, the way they appear
and disappear but go nowhere.

Visitation Rites

We meet at the bookstore
Saturday afternoons
for lattes and cannoli. I ask
after their week at school
and they tell me about mock
trials, state capitols, Hitler
and World War II; the new kids
who might become their friends.

They eat ravenously, and I
torture myself imagining
they are starved for love.
They wipe their mouths,
fold their napkins, thank me
too sincerely, then drift off
to nooks and are subsumed.

Each week, they seem taller,
more angular, the softness
disappearing from their bodies
the way the down did
when they were born, their skin
as thin as the scrim that separates
our lives from the shadows
they cast, backlit, for all the world

to see, as if this were a play we might
get right another night, and not
their one and only childhood,
my one and only chance to control
the damage, stave the blood-letting

that commenced when first
the cords were severed
and it ceased to be enough
to carry them, breathe for them,
allow them to feed off my flesh
as I would even still if it could be
that simple, if self-sacrifice were sufficient
and it wasn't also essential to survive.

It is one thing to die
for our sins, and another to live
with them, day in and day out,
enacting the ritual of transubstantiation
in all its inadequate glory.

Before I know it, their father
returns to reclaim them,
and I am gathering up the crumbs,
I am putting away the cups.

July 1st

It is the anniversary of a marriage
that did not last, but it is not the birthday
of a dead child, and neither of us
is in anguish anymore.

The temperatures outside are breaking
records, but we are in our separate,
temperate homes, performing chores,
taking turns with the children
who have survived: the eldest just back
from his first solo flight; the middle
newly in love with the surf; the youngest
just trying, like the rest of us, to keep pace
with the world whirling around him—a blur

of computer screens and commuter traffic
where once there was, among other things,
a field of daisies on a mild morning,
many years ago in a faraway state,
and I picked some and swaddled them
in my grandmother's monogrammed
handkerchief, and a doe crossed our path
on the way to the magistrate, and though
it happened all the time, we took it as a sign,
unable to conceive of what it might portend,
or that an end would come, and look like this,
or anything.

That They Need Nothing from Us

Now that I think I've begun to begin
to fathom something of devotion,
I wonder if there is anything I can do
to make up for having ruined your life.

A bottle of wine seems inadequate, somehow,
especially since you've quit drinking,
and it occurs to me that this is the trouble
with the old and the dead, and with God,
for that matter: that they need nothing
from us, not even our gratitude, not even
an apology for our ingratitude.

When in A Quiet Moment

When, in a quiet moment,
I imagine you dead
or dying—that final failure,
the disappointment of it all—
a gentle feeling comes, and I want
to undo our undoing, as I do
when I see our sons rise
to the occasion we have staged for them,
building their characters
like monuments to resilience and not
our flesh and blood, the one task
asked of us answered
so pathetically, as if it were about us.

I imagine you remembering
your long life, shaking your head
at the thought that you ever thought
it was within reason to hope.

I imagine touching the soft folds
of your face again—as in the beginning,
so in the end: uttering with love
the lies we long to be told
and so tell ourselves.

Something to Be Said

Almost without effort, every end can be
foreseen—each season's and each story's;
the end of all things suffered and of each
fleeting ecstasy; childbirth's end
but also childhood's; the nightmare's end,
but also the dream's.

The sunrise you rose early to see,
and the fire you couldn't bear to watch;
the long marriage, and the affair
you knew better than to have—each
of these, played out in your head,
amounts to nothing.

Why bother, then, to get out of bed
unless there is, as there must be,
something to be said
for showing up and submitting ourselves
to the boredom and the bliss,
the interminable caress, the excruciating kiss

of existence here, where it is not enough
to hypothesize and extrapolate, even if
the outcome remains the same. We must
stay present, pay attention and let
our bodies know these moments,
record them in our cells and souls—

the clock ticking on the wall,
the smell of woodsmoke and old books;
sunburn, and the icy chill
of going under; waves
of pressure building until
you think you will implode, then

breaking, as a cloud releases rain,
the baby laid across your chest,
bare skin to bare skin, flesh
of your flesh, his perfect hand
wrapped 'round your finger
like a wedding band.

The light on the horizon,
diffuse at first, cuts through
the silence like a cry
that fills the sky with flames.
The years are stones,
and love, the fence
we build of them, piece
by piece, fitting each slate
against the next, keeping them
close, though between the cracks
bright lichen grows,
intricate and unimaginable.

Part VI: Abiding

I'm Not Making This Up

Somewhere along the interstate
between my old life and the new,
I come upon a hearse marked "Gamble"
on a placard in the back window
and wonder if and how
I'm supposed to interpret
this dream—the one in which I'm seeking
higher ground, fleeing the flood-
plain for the mountains, familiar
perils for certain death—

                              for death *is*

certain, sooner or later, yours
and mine, and I'm afraid
I won't be able to make it
back to you in time, that you'll die
alone as I found you, reasonably
content but not
ecstatic, as we were
together, briefly, every
love song ours to sing
along to in the jeep, the rag-
top down, or dance to
around the living room,
and you would sometimes
say, with tears in your eyes,
I'm so happy, as if you were
surprised, as if you knew

it would not last—

                      though to be fair,
you've said the same with equal feeling
before meals of bread and cheese,
a bottle of red wine
breathing, the evening sun in the trees.

One Particular Tree

My father has come
to the rescue again: driven
twelve hours south
with a trunk full of tools—
power drill, pickaxe, circular
saw—to help mend my broken
life.
      First, he hangs pictures—
art in the dining room, family
photos upstairs—then he builds
a compost coop of chicken wire
and two-by-fours for the kitchen scraps
I generate en masse, squandering what little
creative energy I have on chickpea soup
with chard, stone fruit crisp with cardamom
and almonds.
      Then he plants herbs—
parsley, sage, cilantro, basil and thyme—
in a galvanized tub my mother scavenged
from the roadside; rosemary, mint
and oregano out front; marigolds
beside the spent daylilies; tomatoes
and peppers and citronella
in terracotta pots; Boston ferns
in hanging baskets, impatiens
on the porch.
      Next he fixes
the ice machine, and I make tea

in mason jars to keep him hydrated
while he mounts outdoor lights
around the back deck, as if we might
entertain some day, celebrate.

      Finally, he begins to rake
a walkway to the carriage house, fills it
with paver's sand and three tons of granite
dumped in the yard from which we're meant
to puzzle out a path, flagstones of all widths
and lengths and he, with one knee
replaced twice, finishes this and then begins
to break up the cracked concrete front walk.

He stays three weeks and scarcely
pauses—paints the fireplace, buys
bird feeders—wakes early and studies
one particular tree, towering.

Dusk

falling in a field
by the French
Broad River.

Storm clouds
gathering
in bundles
of ink and bruise,
streaked with light.

Three of my four
children reunited,
the eldest catching fire-
flies in his cupped palms,
he claims, for the first
time in his life.

We take cover
just in time:

The sky opens;
flashes of lightning
illuminate
sheets of rain.

Inside, thunder shakes
this new old house.

Lamps flicker.
I make nettle-
leaf tea and rub
my youngest son's
growing legs
with menthol
and camphor.

All night
the baby turns
cartwheels in her dreams.

Rites of Spring

I.

First I water the ferns
I've tried to keep alive
all winter. Each time
frost was forecast
I carried them
from the front porch,
through the house and down
to the basement, hung them
from gas lines that criss-
cross the low-slung ceilings
there, left them in the dark
(for weeks on end unwatered,
but relatively warm),
then carried them
back up and out
for every thaw.

I use the long-necked can to reach
deep into the tangled fronds.
My two-year-old stands beneath
the hanging baskets, watches
and waits for overflow to seep
through the base and rain
down on her hands, her face
a shower of laughter blooming
as she splashes and laps,

all delight and yet
I wonder
if they will in fact survive,
so many leaves lost, so many others
desiccated and scattering
in the wind even now, as if
they were petals and not
the detritus of last year's Mother's Day gift,
so lush in the beginning, so green
against the white-washed clapboard
in the shade all summer long.

II.

On the back deck, I fill a tub
with tepid tap water, let my daughter
undress and soak in the sun,
draw a comb through her wet hair,
sleek as a river otter, as I became
nights my own mother drew
a bath and dimmed the lights,
allowed me to luxuriate
in the weightlessness of the buoyant
body she must have known
would not last.

Across the alley, a man
practices guitar in his yard,
strumming simple chords
in chorus with the thrum
of the neighborhood repairing itself

after the ordinary ravages of winter—
downed limbs, loose bricks,
weeds reclaiming the territory
our gardens were only ever occupiers of.

The child is oblivious
to all of this, focused instead
on the way her sieve holds water
for only a moment, then shatters it
into a billion beads of liquid light.

III.

Inside, I stem strawberries,
snap the ends off asparagus
and steam them just long enough
to draw out their wild grassiness,
like that of the fiddleheads
and leeks I learned to forage
when I was young and morels
multiplied in the musty humus,
their sacred hiding places still secret.

After lunch, we walk to the park
to play. Puddles from last week's
rains remain beneath the swings,
the slides. Dandelions abound
on the surrounding slopes,
brilliant yellow suns, or in a later state:
nebulous, wishful, almost invisible.

IV.

After a week,
I take the spade
my mother gave me
and dig a grave
the size and shape
of the root-bound
urn filler, sword fern,
Nephrolepis exaltata,
invert it like a newborn
onto my open palm, then lay it back
into the ground,
tamp the earth around
what's left above
and turn the sprinkler on.

It will be killed by cold,
I'm told, but then,
come spring, rebound.

Yellow Jackets

When my fifteen year-old is diagnosed
(after screaming in the kitchen,
pulling fistfuls of hair, banging
my head against the bathroom door),
I set about reorganizing my twelve
year-old's bedroom: Position the head-
board to afford a better view, trade out
his rickety dresser, scavenged from the road-
side, for a newer, smoother one. Likewise
a bookcase—

        this way, his things
can be less crowded, more orderly,
less likely to tangle or tear—

        And I am aware
I am trying to save him, myself,
control what I can control,
hold on for dear life—

        for life *is* dear,
Dear, and we are as delicate as the dead
yellow jackets I gather
from the window sills: Desiccated, no longer
dangerous, but innumerable,
and we have no idea
where they're coming from—

        And I pray
the medication will and won't
change him, just lift the anvil,
penetrate the dark—

(Their stripes are so
precise; their wings like dry
petals of tiny flowers, their bodies
weightless in my palm,
by the least breeze made
animate, as if they were
still buzzing, still thirsty, still
capable of flight.)
                         I leave a light on,
nights—the front door unlocked,
leftovers in a pot on the stovetop—

in case he's hungry
when he comes home. In case
he comes home.

Homecoming

Not since I was last in love
have I said I'd just as soon
stay in and meant it:
               The clothes
I've worn all day are warm
and comfortable, the air
too cool to want to change,
the dog beside me snoring soothingly,
the food in the next room
sufficient unto me.
              This book
as much companionship
as I could hope, as bright
and flattering as any light;
this wine as fine as I can tell,
the quiet more amenable
than any throng.
              We labor long
to dodge the demons of our solitude,
believing them anathema
to love, but they are angels,
too, if we can see them so,
beating their wings
against our hearts' glass cases,
begging to break into them.

I Am Trying to Heed

I am trying to heed
your advice: to keep
(or cultivate, as the case may be)
a sense of humor.
                  I begin
with research: read up
on the evolutionary psychology
of laughter, a signal to ourselves
and others, it is said,
that whatever horror
we've encountered isn't
as threatening as it appears.

Then I start writing
an essay but it isn't
funny at all. I can't
seem to make light,
which is to say, *radiant energy*,
which is to say, *a small segment
of the electromagnetic spectrum*—
of waking, that morning,
to an email on my phone
from the man asleep
beside me, our three-year-old
daughter dreaming between us,
telling me we're through.

But perhaps I'm not trying
hard enough, not
sufficiently practiced
in the arts of slapstick and self-
deprecation, irony and farce, perhaps
it's a matter of making a habit,
(taking a habit? like that of a nun)
of tripping before we are
pushed, admitting our faults
and flaws before they can be
pointed out, and doing so
so straight-faced and deadpan
no one imagines
it's all been a joke.

Aubade

for Matt

The birds have not lost
their religion: they sing

to make the sun rise
every morning, a chorus

at the forest's edge,
on the mountaintop

where the dawn can be
seen to overtake the dark,

first light illuminating
February's golden grasses

against the gray sky, growing
gradually pale until

the clouds blush,
bouquets of carnations tossed

toward the heavens, hopeless
romantic that this planet is:

ready to give
each day its dowry

despite the unlikelihood
that it will have her.

And the birds, the birds
bestow their blessing.

About the Author

Brit Washburn was born and raised in Northern Michigan, and educated at Interlochen Arts Academy, The New School, University of Hawaii, and Goddard College. She works as a writer, editor, indexer, cook, and baker, and lives with her four children in Asheville, North Carolina. Her poems and essays can be found in various magazines, journals and reviews, and at *www.theoryandpracticeofbeing.wordpress.com*, which consists of a reader's reflections on religion and relationship, with recipes.

Wet Cement Press Books

Thoreau Lovell
Wilson Wiley Variations
ISBN 978-1-7324369-1-6

Michelle Murphy
Synonym for Home
ISBN 978-1-7324369-2-3

Barbara Roether
Saraswati's Lament
ISBN 978-1-7324369-0-9

Anthony Schlagel
My Dog, Me
ISBN 978-1-7324369-3-0

Brit Washburn
Notwithstanding
ISBN 978-1-7324369-5-4